D1121586

The Scientist's
Guide to Physics™

Discovering the
Construct
of
Time

JOHNNY KAGAYAME
AND JOSEPHA SHERMAN

ROSEN
PUBLISHING®

New York

Published in 2012 by The Rosen Publishing Group, Inc.
29 East 21st Street, New York, NY 10010

Library of Congress Cataloging-in-Publication Data

Kagayame, Johnny.
Discovering the construct of time / Johnny Kagayame, Josepha Sherman.—1st ed.
    p. cm.—(The scientist's guide to physics)
Includes bibliographical references and index.
ISBN 978-1-4488-4703-7 (lib. bdg.)
1. Space and time—Juvenile literature. I. Sherman, Josepha. II. Title.
QC173.59.S65K34 2012
529—dc22

                                        2010042035

Manufactured in the United States of America

CPSIA Compliance Information: Batch #S11YA: For further information, contact Rosen Publishing, New York, New York, at 1-800-237-9932.

Contents

INTRODUCTION

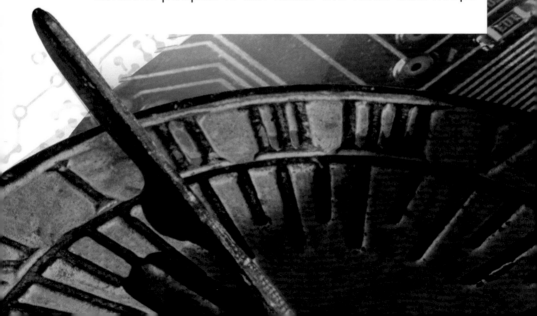

The concept of time is both fluid and concrete. Its passing is evident when the sun rises and sets and the stars move across the sky, when we feel the seasons change, and we watch as people age year after year. But it is also intangible—one person says, "I'm having the time of my life," and another says, "I have time on my hands." Here time is an abstract idea, more than just an unvarying stream from the past through the present and on to the future.

The word "time" can mean different things to different people. It can mean the force that keeps events in motion. It can also mean a passage between events or a specific number of minutes, hours, or days. In fact, not everybody agrees on how time operates. Some cultures, including our own North American and European ones, believe in "linear time." That is, we see time as a river, something that keeps steadily flowing from point A down to point Z, without ever going from point Z back "upstream" again. Other cultures, such as those influenced by Buddhism and Hinduism, see time as cyclical. Everything that once happened will happen again. In Hindu belief, creation is cyclical and never ending. Each cycle has four great yugas, or epochs of time: Satya yuga, Treta yuga, Dwapar yuga, and Kali yuga, lasting from four thousand years to one thousand years, respectively. Time and creation then "begin to end and end to begin."

Whatever time may actually be, it seems likely that for as far back as human beings have been aware, people have realized that there were such things as time and the passage of time. The earliest measurements of time would have likely been the most obvious: the way that the sun, the moon, and the stars and planets seem to move across the sky. One of the obvious measurements would surely have been a solar year, which is the time that it takes for the earth to revolve around the sun. In addition, the changing shape of the moon would also have given human observers an easy way to keep track of time. The moon waxes and wanes on a regular schedule, from new moon (completely dark) to first quarter (half moon) to full moon and back again every 29.5 days, the division that would eventually be called a month. From early humans to present day, the stars have been a key element in understanding time. To make sense of the construct of time, let's start by looking to the past to our ancestors and their rudimentary timekeeping.

EARLY TIMEKEEPING

Chapter

1

Thirty thousand years ago, early humans weren't worried about missing the bus because their alarms didn't go off, being late to homeroom, or forgetting to set the time on their TiVos. Their concept of time, and their way of life, was very different than ours today. It would have been important for those early humans to know the length of the days and the changing of the seasons. They would have had to know when the animals they needed to hunt for food would migrate or have offspring. They would also have had to know when the plants they ate would bear seeds or fruit. Early humans were nomadic, which means they followed herds and traveled from place to place in search of food. Since they traveled

These bone plaques are believed to be early calendars. Found in Israel, they date back to 800–100 BCE.

on foot, whatever they carried had to be lightweight. This would include any way to keep track of time. Carved bones found in Europe and Asia that have been dated as thirty thousand years old may have been early forms of pocket calendars. These carvings seem to have been worked deliberately to show a lunar month—a month based on the time it takes for the moon to go through a cycle of waxing and waning. They are the perfect size for a human to easily carry or wear.

But as time passed, the nomadic lifestyle waned and complex civilizations began to develop. City-states with large populations dependent on organized agriculture appeared. Knowing the time became more important to people, since they had to plan the planting and harvesting of their food supplies. Not only were years and months used for measuring time, but more specific points in the year were noted: the two major solstices, summer and winter, and two equinoxes, vernal (spring) and autumnal.

The summer solstice occurs near June 21 on our modern calendar. It is the time when the sun is at its northernmost point in our sky. This is the longest day of the year. The winter solstice occurs near December 21, when the sun reaches its southernmost point in our sky. This is the shortest day of the year. In the Northern Hemisphere, the vernal, or spring, equinox occurs near March 20, when the sun passes the equator from south to north. On the vernal equinox, day and night are approximately the same lengths. The autumnal equinox occurs around September 22, when the sun passes the equator from north to south. Once again, as with the vernal equinox, day and night are approximately the same lengths.

ANCIENT TIMEKEEPERS

Around 3000 BCE, in the civilization of ancient Sumer in Mesopotamia—in what is now Iraq—the Sumerians created a twelve-month calendar. Their months were based on lunar phases. They also divided the year into two seasons. The dry season was called *emesh*.

It began around February or March. The wet season, *enten*, began in September or October, with the arrival of the rains.

At about the same time, the civilization of the ancient Egyptians was growing along the Nile River. Although Egypt is mostly a desert land, every year the Nile flooded, bringing fertile mud onto the fields and making good harvests possible. Around 3000 BCE, Egyptian astronomers noted that the first rising of the star Sirius in the morning sky marked the time that the Nile's flooding usually began. By about 1100 BCE, they had created a catalog of what they could see of the universe with the naked eye. It included a list of star groups known as *decans*. The decans were useful for keeping track of time: each star's rising at night marked the start of the next hour. Several wooden sarcophagi, or coffins, from about 2000 BCE show diagrams that may have been solar clocks tracking the decans to tell time at night. Some of the Egyptian tombs from about 1400 BCE have painted ceilings that not only provide a chart of the decans but of the lunar months as well.

Working with the information they had about the movements of the heavens and the lengths of days, Egyptian astronomers devised a calendar of 365 days, with twelve months. Each month was made up of thirty days. Since the actual year doesn't divide evenly, there was extra time left over in the Egyptian

THE KARNAK CLEPSYDRA

[AMENOPHIS III : CIRCA 1400 B.C]

CELESTIAL DIAGRAM ON EXTERIOR SURFACE

SMALL RESTORATIONS, FROM CEILING OF TOMB OF SENMUT [1500 BC] & RAMESSEUM [1260 BC]

calendar once every four years, the way there is with our modern leap year. They had three seasons: *ache*, or flooding, *proje*, or winter, and *schomu*, or summer.

The Egyptians also kept track of time with sundials and water clocks. Sundials are circles marked at regular points with a raised marker. As the sunlight travels over the clock, the shadow created by the marker points to the time. Water clocks don't rely on

HERBERT CHATLEY
D.S., M.Inst.C.E.

This hieroglyphic celestial diagram was copied from the Karnak clepsydra, or water clock, that was uncovered in the Temple of Karnak, in Luxor, Egypt. The original artifact dates back to 1415–1380 BCE.

sunlight. A water clock measures time by the regulated dropping of water from one bowl to another or from one bowl out onto the ground. Both sundials and water clocks date to about 1500 BCE. The idea that the ancient Egyptians considered keeping time important can be assumed from the fact that a water clock was found in the tomb of Pharaoh Amenhotep I, who died around 1500 BCE.

WATER CLOCKS

After the Egyptians, the next major civilization to make use of water clocks was ancient Greece. The Greeks started using water clocks around the fourth century BCE and dubbed the devices clepsydras, or water thieves, since the water was stolen from the bowls. Greek clepsydras were usually made of stone or metal, and they usually had sloping sides. Each water clock had a small hole at the bottom, out of which water could drip (or be "stolen" by gravity) at a nearly constant rate. Markings on the insides of the bowls showed the passing of time as the water level fell.

By the end of the first century BCE and into the first century CE, both the Greeks and the Romans began developing more elaborate, mechanized water clocks. The designers of these more modern devices were trying to make the flow of the water more constant by regulating the water pressure. But the new designs also put on quite a show for the viewer. Some water clocks rang bells or struck gongs. Others opened tiny windows to show little figures of people. Still others moved pointers or even featured models of the universe as the ancients understood it.

The most exotic of these mechanical water clock devices was the eight-sided Horologion, also known as the Tower of the Winds. A Macedonian astronomer, Andronikos, erected the Horologion in the Athenian marketplace in the first century BCE. The Horologion had a twenty-four-hour mechanized clepsydra, eight sundials (one on each of its eight sides), pointers for the eight winds—which gave the tower its name—and indicators of the seasons of the year and important astronomical dates and periods.

From about 200 CE on, the Chinese devised water clocks that powered various astronomical machines. Su Sung, a Chinese designer, was commissioned to build the most exotic of these in 1086 CE. His machine included a clock tower that was over 30 feet (9.1 meters) tall, a continually revolving globe, and moving figurines that struck gongs.

GREEK OBSERVATIONS AND EXPERIMENTS

Looking for more accurate ways to tell time, the Greeks also designed different styles of sundials. In addition to the standard flat sundial, there was also the hemicycle, which was shaped like half a bowl. In fact, by about 30 BCE, there were at least thirteen different styles of sundial being used throughout Greece and Italy.

The Greeks used the motion of the stars in time-keeping as well. Proof of this comes in the *Works and Days* of Hesiod, an early Greek poet who lived and wrote around 700 BCE. He gives farmers information about the times for plowing and harvesting, writing that when the Pleiades (a cluster of stars in the constellation Taurus) rise it is time to use the sickle. But when the Pleiades are setting, the plough should be used, and when the star Arcturus can be seen at dawn, it is time to pick grapes.

The Greek calendar was a lunar one, and that eventually led to problems when the Greeks tried to link it to solar time. By 600 BCE, an early calendar of twelve months of thirty days each had failed and been replaced by one with six thirty-day full months and six twenty-nine-day empty months. But that one failed as well. The Greek statesman Solon, who lived in the sixth century BCE, also tried his hand at creating an improved calendar. He, too, failed. The Greek astronomer Meton invented yet another calendar, this time in 432 BCE, but his doesn't seem to have been put into public use. Meton and another astronomer, Euctemon, are known for their invention of the *parapegma*, a stone tablet with pegs that could be moved to match the movement of the stars

These are the remains of an early portable sundial with gears to operate the calendar. The outer ring is inscribed with Greek towns and their latitudes. These would have been used to calibrate the instrument.

with special dates. Parapegmai were also made out of papyrus, a type of reed paper from Egypt that was used before the invention of wood pulp paper.

MORE TRIAL AND ERROR: THE FORMATION OF THE ROMAN CALENDAR

For all these exotic and not quite accurate ways of counting the hours, counting the days and years had become a true problem for the Romans. Their calendars were confusing and inaccurate. They counted the beginning of the month from first sighting of the moon's crescent after the new moon. But they measured the year with a solar calendar. This meant that every four years, there were too many days. By 46 BCE, the Roman calendar was off by about three months.

This lack of accuracy was definitely not good enough for the Roman dictator Julius Caesar. He commissioned Sosigenes, an astronomer from Alexandria, Egypt, to design a calendar that was both more accurate and simpler to use. Sosigenes did his calculations and came up with a year having a length of 365.25 days. He divided this figure into twelve months and gave the months thirty or thirty-one days apiece. This left the problem of the leap year, the

Julius Caesar, depicted on this gold coin circa 46 BCE, was not satisfied with Rome's inaccurate calendars. He called for a new calendar—one simpler and more precise—to be designed.

extra time that doesn't fit into the regular scheme. This extra time seems to have been a little too much for Sosigenes, who miscalculated it as being necessary every third year instead of every fourth year. As a result, inaccuracies were bound to creep into his calendar, even though Augustus Caesar, who followed Julius, saw to it that the leap year was calculated every four years. By this point, the new calendar worked very well, especially compared to what had come before. What Sosigenes had devised is known as the Julian calendar, after the man who commissioned it. The Julian calendar remained in use for centuries, and it is still used by some of the Orthodox Christian churches around the world for the setting of feast days.

Even some lunar calendars are still in use in the world today, though usually not as a primary way of keeping track of time. The modern Jewish calendar, for instance, is a lunar one, and as a result, Jewish holidays fall on different days of the common calendar each year. Some Islamic countries, such as Saudi Arabia, use a lunar calendar as well.

TIME IN EAST ASIA

Meanwhile, efforts to keep track of time were well underway in East Asia, particularly in China where they had developed a calendar, as well. The Chinese calendar was very complicated. There, the calendar was considered a sacred link between heaven and the ruling emperor. A special bureau of astronomy was in charge of the maintenance of the calendar. When a new ruler came to the throne, a new era began, with the year count starting from day one of the new reign. But an emperor could also declare the start of a new era after a natural disaster or a solar eclipse.

The earliest Chinese calendars of which we have records date to the Shang dynasty of the fourteenth century BCE. They had two different forms of monthly cycles, one using a lunar system and the other using a solar one. The year was divided into twenty-four segments. The new year was originally marked at the time of the new moon nearest the winter solstice, but a calendar reform in the second century BCE set the calendar so that the winter solstice happened during the eleventh month. There were still problems, though, in matching up the solar and lunar calendars, and those remained unsolved until modern times.

THE NEW WORLD
KEEPS ITS EYES ON THE STARS

In the New World, the Maya of Central America built a civilization that lasted from about 2600 BCE to 900

CE. The Maya had a strong interest in astronomy, as it was tied to timekeeping, the rhythms of agriculture, and religion. Without the technology or materials with which to build telescopes, they were forced to rely on their eyes. But they built sophisticated observatories and made use of shadow-casting devices, such as straight sticks, to let them trace the path of the sun. Rituals were carried out to ensure that the predictable cycles of the sky would continue.

The Maya used not just the sun and moon but also the planet Venus in designing a complex calendar. The Mayan year consisted of 360 days and each day had a name. The glyph (symbol) *kin* meant one day. *Winal* was a collection of twenty days, or a month. *Tun* was the glyph for a year, and *k'atun* was a time period of twenty years of 360 days each. A *baktun* was an epoch of four hundred years.

The Aztec culture of Mexico, centered in what is now Mexico City, lasted

This colored illustration depicts the Aztec sun stone calendar. The calendar contains a 365-day year and a 260-day ritual cycle.

from about 900 CE to 1517, when it was ended violently by the Spanish invasion from Europe. The Aztecs had a calendar as complex as that of the Maya. An Aztec year was made up of eighteen months and added up to 360 days. The five extra days were called *nemontemi*. They were thought to be unlucky and were days of sacrifice—often human. The Aztecs created enormous calendar stones carved in intricate relief. These stones seem to have served them both as ritual calendars and sundials. Whether or not the Aztecs thought of time as linear—flowing in a straight line—or circular isn't clear. There is some evidence for both ideas. It is known, though, that the Aztecs did give specific values to every day, year, and collection of years. They believed that the entire intricate passage of time needed specially timed offerings or sacrifices—of plants, animals, or humans—if it was all to keep operating properly.

In South America, a people known as the Inca took over most of the western half of the continent, along the Andes mountain range. The Inca Empire lasted from 1438 until 1536, when, like the empire of the Aztecs, Spanish invaders conquered it. The Incan calendar, like that of the Maya, was based on the movements of the sun, the moon, and the stars. There is little information about the details of the calendar, although there were apparently twelve months tied into the agricultural cycle. The Inca also organized their work using six weeks of nine days each.

As human civilizations continued to advance, so did the need for more accurate timekeeping methods. Religious and economic factors may have been the spark for these technological advancements, but for a great many innovators and inventors, it was the desire itself to harness and understand time, just like the ancient timekeepers that came before them. This refined measurement of time was to be a slow process.

CHRONOLOGY OF TIME

Chapter

2

People living during the European Middle Ages (about 500–1500 CE) still looked to the sky for guidance on the time of day or the time of year. Until the beginning of the Renaissance, ordinary people simply didn't concern themselves with time except to determine the right season for planting or harvesting or knowing when a festival might occur.

THE CHURCH AND TIME

The Catholic Church, however, was more concerned with time. Its scholars were busy working out the time of biblical events such as the Creation, and they were also concerned about Judgment Day, when the world as they knew it was supposed to end. Before the fifth century CE, the common belief in western Europe was that the world would exist for only six thousand years, and this led to a great interest in what things would be like afterward. This interest lasted up through the end of the first millennium CE. In 1000 CE, in fact, many people did think that the end of the world had come and waited on hilltops all night for the Lord's final judgment. They had interpreted various events at the time as the fulfilling of the prophecy of Christ's return, including the fall of the Holy Roman Empire. When, instead, the sun rose as usual on the next morning, they must have felt sheepish, relieved, or both as they returned to their homes and work. But they weren't the only ones to be fooled like this. Some people at the end of the nineteenth century also believed that time had run out. They also went up onto hilltops to pray and wait for the end of the world all night and then went home, happy or disappointed, when sunrise came as usual.

No one is sure when the first mechanical clock was invented. One possible inventor may have been Pacificus, the archdeacon of Verona, who was born about 776 and died about 844. He was a learned scholar and an astronomer as well as a churchman.

Pacificus is said to have built some type of clock in the early ninth century, but not much else is known about it or what happened to it.

Another candidate for creator of the first mechanical clock is Pope Sylvester II, who was originally a monk named Gerbert. Born around 940 or 950, the pope was a highly educated scholar, skilled in several fields. The pope is often credited with the invention of a mechanical clock around 996 CE. But again, as with the story about Pacificus, there is no real proof of this. Pope Sylvester II died on May 12, 1003, without leaving any writing about clocks.

There is more tangible evidence of clock-making skills from the end of the thirteenth century. A clock was installed in St. Paul's Cathedral in London in 1286. The most entertaining part of the clock was the mechanical figures that struck a bell on the hour. Another clock was placed in a tower at Westminster Hall, London, in 1288. A third clock was added to Canterbury Cathedral in 1292.

Such clocks, though, were very rare, since they were large and expensive. They were also not very

The bell tower of St. Paul's Cathedral in London, England, as it appears today. St. Paul's Cathedral was home to one of the earliest mechanical clocks in the world.

accurate. That didn't matter, though; ordinary people of the thirteenth century still weren't worrying very much about the concepts of past or future. They simply reckoned time by major events, like the crowning of a new king or the time of a great storm. After all, it wasn't necessary for someone to know the specific hour if he or she worked on a farm. The times necessary for peasants—knowing when to plant and when to harvest—could be learned from the changing seasons.

TIMEKEEPING ARISES FROM ECONOMIC NECESSITY

By the fourteenth century, as more and more people moved into cities and became trade craftsmen, merely glancing at a sundial or saying, "It happened on the first day of King Stephen's reign," was no longer enough. A middle class of merchants and small-scale manufacturers appeared, and these people employed many others in workshops and home handicraft production. Manufacturers had to measure the value of time spent producing goods. Merchants and bankers needed to measure accurately the duration of loans, the interest earned on them over time, and how long it would take to ship goods from one port to another. Increasingly, people needed to know more precisely what time it was, and they needed to divide their day into specific hours. And as the methods of science began to become more widely accepted, there was a greater need for more precise measurement of time in experiments.

This need for more detailed ways to tell time marks the beginning of the true age of mechanical clocks. The first of these more modern clocks appeared during the first half of the fourteenth century, and they were installed in the towers of Italian cities. These clocks were fairly simple devices, driven by weight or, more specifically, gravity. They were relatively accurate due to what is called a verge-and-foliot escapement.

The verge of such a clock is a central vertical shaft within the body of the clock. The foliot is a freely swinging horizontal bar attached to it. The escapement is the wheel in a clock that keeps the pendulum moving by allowing a tooth of cogged wheel to escape with each move. A pendulum is anything that is suspended from a fixed support so that it constantly oscillates, or swings freely back and forth, under the influence of gravity. Also within the body of such a clock is a horizontal spindle

with a cord wrapped around it. A weight hangs from the cord. As gravity slowly pulls the weight down, the cord unwinds, turning the spindle. A gear on the spindle makes the escapement and the verge and foliot vibrate. At the same time, the escapement regulates the rate at which the spindle turns. The turning of the spindle moves a hand around the face of the clock.

An odd side effect of the coming of mechanical clocks was the separation of clock time from solar and lunar time. For the first time, people were looking to a machine to measure time, rather than consulting the position of the sun. Using mechanical clocks to measure time was very different from using natural events such as the sunrise or the vernal equinox. The movements of celestial bodies are subject to all sorts of real or apparent irregularities, depending upon long-term changes in the movements of the earth or the location of the observer on its surface. Now mechanical clocks imposed an inflexible regularity on time, abstracting it from the motion of the universe.

The Salisbury Cathedral clock, in Salisbury, England, is the oldest working clock in the world, dating back to about 1386. The mechanism shows the crown wheel and the foliot, at top supporting stone weights.

These clocks were still only relatively accurate, since there was no way to perfectly control the vibration of the escapement. Despite their lack of accuracy, though, clocks of the fourteenth century were often elaborate affairs. In 1352, a clock was placed in the cathedral of Strasbourg, Germany, that was truly amazing. It showed the current positions of the sun, moon, and other heavenly bodies in addition to the time of day. The clock had elaborate mechanical figures that included the twelve apostles, a crowing rooster, a revolving celestial globe, and an automatic calendar dial.

INTRODUCING THE SPRING-POWERED CLOCK: SIXTEENTH-CENTURY ACHIEVEMENTS

The next great advance in clock design came in the sixteenth century from Peter Henlein of Nuremberg, Germany. Born around 1480, he became a master locksmith in 1509. Although very little is known about his life and career, he eventually developed the spring-powered clock. Unlike the verge-and-foliot clocks, which were generally very large, the spring clocks could be of any size. Getting rid of those bulky,

LATITUDE AND LONGITUDE

Until the fifteenth century, almost everyone lived by local time. It's easy to think like this: noon exists only for me and the people around me. But after the first successful voyage of Christopher Columbus in 1492, people were forced to realize that the world was too large for only local time to apply. Noon happened at different times in different places around the world.

The Portuguese mapmaker Pedro Reinel was the first to puzzle out a solution to the problem of time and navigation over distance. He simply broke up the distance into segments of local time. In 1506, he became the first person to draw a latitude scale on a prime meridian, an arbitrary north-south line that divided up time and space over the globe and the sky. Latitude lines run east to west and divide the globe into horizontal segments. But the Portuguese mapmakers knew that they needed to establish longitude as well.

Longitude lines run north to south, and they are the important dividers of local time. By the 1520s, the Portuguese knew that only a truly accurate clock would be able to solve the problem of accurately measuring longitude. There was no such clock yet.

heavy escapements and spindles meant that smaller clocks and even pocket watches could now be built. The wealthy eagerly bought these smaller clocks, delighted to have a timepiece that could actually be kept on a table or mantle. Henlein died a wealthy man in 1542. But it still wasn't a truly accurate clock, as it would slow as the mainspring unwound.

Forty years later, in 1582, there was an improvement to the Western calendar as well. Pope Gregory XIII commissioned an improved version. This time, the problems surrounding the creation and proper placement of the leap year were solved. This corrected calendar was named after the pope who'd commissioned it, and it became known as the Gregorian calendar. The Gregorian calendar is still in use in the Western world today.

ADVANCEMENTS IN THE SEVENTEENTH CENTURY

In 1602, the famous Italian scientist Galileo Galilei (1564–1642) turned his attention to a theory of motion. In 1604, he noted that a pendulum took just as long to make a wide arc as it did to swing through a small arc, and he saw the possibility of using pendulum theory to make a better clock. But he died without having ever designed such a clock or even having published his work on pendulums.

A few years after Galileo's death, Dutch astronomer and mathematician Christian Huygens (1629–1695) began working on the physics of pendulums as part of his mathematical studies. He knew that the science of astronomy needed accurate timekeeping, and he began designing a clock. In 1656, Huygens patented the world's first pendulum clock. It was the most accurate clock yet, off by less than a minute a day. Huygens built several pendulum clocks to determine longitude, and they were tried aboard ships at sea in 1662 and again in 1686. But the motion of the sea threw off the accuracy of his clocks. He described his findings in *Horologium Oscillatorium sive de Motu Pendulorum*, published in 1673.

Seventeenth-century clocks came to have various names, all depending on the look of their cases. There were birdcage clocks, lantern clocks, and sheep's-head clocks. Most of these cases were made of wood or brass. Most had bells or small gongs at the top to strike the hours. Colonists who immigrated to America, particularly to New England and Virginia, took such clocks with them, and they became common possessions as the colonies grew. About this time, clocks that had long cases were developed. These were made of wood and hid the

long pendulums that kept them going. They were the ancestors of grandfather clocks. By the end of the seventeenth century, these long cases of wood were often beautifully inlaid or ornamented with brass or gold.

By 1671, a new type of escapement had been created. It was called the anchor escapement because it hung like an anchor. It swung back and forth with the pendulum of the clock, with each swing either catching or releasing the clock's wheel. This regular action made pendulum clocks even more dependable. They were able, for the first time, to count minutes and even seconds. One of those working with anchor escapement clocks was Robert Hooke (1635–1703), an English architect, inventor, and scientist. Around 1657, he designed and patented the first anchor escapement clock, although whether or not Hooke actually invented the anchor escapement is disputed.

Hooke's name is also linked to another aspect of time. Fossils and geology also fascinated him. In the seventeenth century, no one was quite sure what

One of the oldest surviving balance spring pocket watches, this pocket watch was made by the great English clock maker Thomas Tompion around 1675. Tompion's clock making was overseen by Robert Hooke.

HOW OLD IS THE EARTH?

Even though the calendar had been corrected, most people around the world still had no idea of geological time, the vast spans of time necessary for the earth to take its present form and for living organisms to evolve. Most people still believed that the earth was only a few thousand years old. Fossils were thought to be the remains of creatures killed in the flood mentioned in the Bible, and this was not thought to have occurred all that long ago. Archbishop James Ussher of Ireland (1581–1656) added up the generations descended from Adam as described in the Old Testament and calculated the age of the earth from that. He wrote in his *Annales veteris testamenti a prima mundi origine deducti* ("The Annals of the Old Testament, Deduced from the First Origin of the World"), published in 1654, that the earth had been created in 4004 BCE. In fact, he stated specifically that the moment of Creation had taken place on October 26, 4004 BCE, at 9:00 AM. This chronology continued to be accepted, at least in western Europe, until the nineteenth century.

fossils were. The problem was made worse by the fact that most people still believed that the earth was only a few thousand years old. Scientists intuitively suspected that this could not be so, but they had no explanation for what fossils were, and they were reluctant to challenge accepted church doctrine. Hooke was the first scientist to examine fossils with a microscope. As a result, he was able to see clear similarities between fossils and living shells, and petrified and living wood. He announced that the fossils were definitely the remains of formerly living shellfish and trees. He was also one of the first scientists to realize that species can become extinct over time. But his ideas were not yet widely accepted. They seemed too strange to be true if the earth was really only a few thousand years old.

In the late seventeenth century, the measurement of longitude remained as much of a problem as it had been for the Portuguese in the early sixteenth century. For every fifteen degrees of longitude that a ship sailed west, the local time for that ship moved back an hour. For every fifteen degrees of longitude that a ship sailed east, its local time moved forward an hour. But if sailors were to accurately calculate their location, they needed to measure their local time against the time at a specific reference point. The difference in time would reflect the distance east or west of the

This oil painting shows Christian Huygens in Salomon Coster's clock maker's shop. The two men are inspecting their first pendulum clock, which was created based on the observations made by Galileo.

prime meridian. Unfortunately, the pendulum clocks of the era could not keep accurate time because of the rolling motions of a ship at sea. King Charles II of England founded the Royal Observatory in 1675 to find a solution to that problem, but for almost fifty years, no solution was found.

EIGHTEENTH-CENTURY CLOCK MAKERS

Timekeeping methods continued to improve into the eighteenth century. George Graham (1674–1751) was a self-taught English astronomer and inventor. Raised by his brother after his father's death, Graham was apprenticed to a London clock maker, Henry Aske, and studied with him from 1688 to 1695. After this apprenticeship, Graham became talented in designing and building precise measuring instruments. He also taught himself astronomy and was even published in scholarly journals. About 1710, he designed a clockwork device that was a model of the earth, the sun, and the planets. The planets moved around the sun as time passed. Constructed for Charles Boyle, the fourth Earl of Orrery, it became known as an orrery. Meanwhile, the designs that Graham created from 1715 to 1755 improved the pendulum clock's accuracy.

John Harrison (1693–1776) was an English carpenter and self-taught clock maker. Harrison had first become intrigued with the idea of building a better timepiece when he was sick as a boy and his parents put a clock on his pillow to amuse him. It was the old-fashioned sort that let him watch the works in action. Harrison built his first clock, made entirely of wood, in 1713. Then, in 1714, the British government

An orrery is a device showing the passage of time represented by the planets and their positions around the sun. This one was presented to Sir Patrick Moore to commemorate his membership in the British Astronomical Association.

offered a challenge. A prize of £20,000 was offered to anyone who could solve the longitude problem. But neither Harrison nor anyone else was ready to claim the prize—not yet.

From 1713 through the mid-1720s, John Harrison and his brother James designed clocks together. Their first success was a clock for a family named Pelham. What made this clock important was that it was the first to need no lubrication, or oiling. This was important because most clock oils of the era were notoriously bad, more likely to foul a clock's works than clean them. The brothers went on to design better and more accurate clocks than any other clock makers in London.

Harrison, however, remained interested in the British government's challenge. By 1761, he had invented

This portrait detail of John Harrison shows the clock maker with his marine chronometer, his greatest achievement. This invention was over forty years in the making.

a marine chronometer that could keep time on board a rolling ship to an accuracy of about one-fifth of a second a day. This won Harrison the prize. However, the Royal Observatory members hated the idea of giving the prize to a nonscientist and someone who didn't even have a college degree. They argued and stalled. It wasn't until 1773 and after years of bitter struggle that Harrison, who finally had to ask for the help of King George III, claimed his reward. Harrison died three years later, in 1776, possibly worn out by his struggle for recognition.

THE SCIENCE OF TIME

Chapter 3

I n the nineteenth century, there was tremendous growth in industrialization, world trade, and scientific knowledge. People were beginning to realize that some global form of timekeeping was necessary. Perhaps the first in the United States to see the growing need for some type of standardization of time measurements was an amateur astronomer named William Lambert. In 1809, he sent a recommendation to this effect to the U.S. Congress, but no one in government at that time was interested in taking up such a project.

Meanwhile, new questions about the actual age of the earth were being raised. Geology, the scientific study of the earth and its rocks and minerals, had started up in the eighteenth century with the basic goal of finding useful minerals for industry. But by the second half of the nineteenth century, the young science of geology had become more sophisticated. Geologists studying the earth raised the possibility that the processes that had shaped the earth had taken not thousands of years but millions and probably billions of years. Archbishop James Ussher had finally been proved wrong. The earth could not have been created in 4004 BCE. It was a great deal older. The question that was bothering scientists now was how old was the earth?

EARTH'S DEVELOPMENT OVER TIME

Englishman Sir Charles Lyell (1797–1875) was one of those interested in proving that the earth had evolved through incredibly long ages, what was beginning to be called geologic time. Lyell developed an early interest in geology, and it became his chosen career. He was deeply influenced by the work of an earlier Scottish geologist, James Hutton (1726–1797). In this three-volume work, *Principles of Geology*, published from 1860 to 1863, Lyell stated that common and well-understood geological processes, still at work, were enough to explain the present form of

Volcanic eruption is one of the ongoing geological processes that Charles Lyell believed was enough to explain how the planet came to have its various features.

the earth. He stated that a combination of the processes of volcanism (earthquakes and volcanic eruptions) and the processes of erosion (the actions of glaciers, water, and wind) was enough to explain the geological features of our planet. At the time, this was known as the uniform series of changes that took place over great lengths of time. Given enough time, incremental changes could account for dramatic geological formations one observed all over the earth.

This theory went against another viewpoint that was popular at the time, the theory of catastrophism. This idea suggested that the earth's geological features had been created suddenly in a series of rapid cataclysmic events, like floods and other major upheavals. Catastrophism did not require the earth to be very old, and this was the favored theory of theologians and conservative thinkers who believed that miracles and divine interventions had given the earth its present form. Lyell and his supporters advocated a vast time-scale for the earth's history and stressed that the age of the human species also had to be far beyond the accepted theories of that time.

EVOLUTION AND THE PASSAGE OF TIME

Lyell's close friend was fellow Englishman Charles Darwin (1809–1882). Darwin was to add a new element to the idea of geologic time through his theory of evolution. This theory stated that living organisms changed with the passage of time, mainly as a result of natural selection, the process by which creatures better adapted to their local environments would reproduce more effectively and survive. All creatures were related to each other through common ancestors in the past, but the creatures alive today looked different from their ancestors and each other

Charles Darwin's theory of evolution helped support Lyell's ideas on the age of the earth and the concept of slow, gradual change resulting in monumental changes over time.

because they had adapted to their environments. In his 1859 book *On the Origin of Species by Means of Natural Selection, or the Preservation of Favoured Races in the Struggle for Life*, known more simply as *The Origin of Species*, Darwin stated that most evolutionary change was gradual, requiring millions or billions of years. Many people were upset by the theory of evolution. They refused to believe that human beings had evolved just like other animals or that humans and other primates were related. The controversy over evolution still continues, but evolution has been accepted by the scientific community and is now considered the fundamental principle of the biological sciences. In any case, Darwin's theory, like Lyell's, required an enormous span of time if incremental changes in the appearance of the earth and the creatures living on it were to take place.

USING THERMODYNAMICS TO DETERMINE THE EARTH'S AGE

In addition to the objections by religious conservatives, there were scientific objections to Lyell's and Darwin's theories. The British physicist Lord Kelvin, who was the leading authority of the time on heat

LORD KELVIN

William Thomson, Baron Kelvin of Largs, was born in present-day Northern Ireland in 1824. He was a physicist, mathematician, and engineer who greatly inspired and influenced his contemporaries.

Though he butted heads with Charles Darwin regarding Darwin's theory of evolution and the geologic age of the earth—Thomson did not have any knowledge about the radioactivity in the planet's core—the strides he made in the field of thermodynamics changed the scientific landscape forever. In a paper published in 1851, he described the second law of thermodynamics, which relates to entropy and increasing disorder in the universe.

Fascinated by heat and energy, Thomson also defined the absolute temperature scale, the unit for which is named after him. He also studied the relationship of electricity and magnetism, inspiring James Clerk Maxwell, who studied Thomson's early works and went on to develop the electromagnetic theory of light.

Thomson's invention of a sensitive mirror galvanometer led to the first successful transatlantic telegraph cable between western Ireland and Newfoundland, Canada, which was laid in 1866. For this achievement, Queen Victoria knighted him.

Lord Kelvin died in Scotland in 1907 and is buried in Westminster Abbey in London.

energy and thermodynamics, assumed that the earth had originally been molten. Knowing all about rates of cooling and heat transfer, he calculated that it had taken no more than 20 to 100 million years for the earth to cool to its present temperature distribution. Though this was still an enormous span of time, it was not enough time for the processes of evolution to take place, and Kelvin's conclusions troubled Darwin. But Kelvin had assumed there was no source of new heat within the Earth. He was wrong.

THE EARTH GETS OLDER

What Kelvin had not considered was the phenomenon of radioactivity. Scientists Pierre and Marie Curie became famous for their research on the radiation given off by chemical elements such as uranium and thorium. British scientist Ernest Rutherford established the nuclear model of the atom and began to theorize about the transmutation of elements when they spontaneously gave off decay particles. The point was that the earth's interior was full of radioactive elements that gave off heat energy in the process of decay. As a result, the earth was not cooling as rapidly as Kelvin thought. It might very well be as old as proposed by Lyell and Darwin.

The first scientific attempts to calculate the age of the earth were based on how long it would take for the total thickness of the sedimentary rocks in the earth's crust to accumulate. Sedimentary rocks are those created from layer after layer of sand and other sediments that accumulate and are compressed by their weight into solid rocks, a process that was thought to occur at a uniform rate. But the strata (layers) of sedimentary rocks vary so greatly in their thickness from area to area that these investigations did not produce useful results. In 1899, an attempt to judge the age of the earth through the salt in the oceans also failed, since salt from land that erodes into the sea is often recycled back into the land.

The work of Rutherford and other scientists on radioactivity, however, had led to the discovery that the rate of radioactive decay of each unstable element is regular. That regular rate of decay could be used, in a technique called radiometric dating, to determine the age of various rocks. In 1913, British geologist Arthur Holmes, who was working on his doctoral degree, proposed the first geological time-scale based on the rates of radioactive decay. He made an estimate of the age of the earth that was far greater than anyone had suggested until then: 4 billion years. That was remarkably close to the age accepted by today's geologists, a little more than 4.5 billion years.

The result of all these investigations was that people were confronted with the idea of a span of time for the existence of living creatures, the earth, and the universe that was unimaginably long, so long that it seemed to render recorded human history almost insignificant by comparison.

CREATING A STANDARD

The accurate measurement of present time was also becoming more and more important. The age of industry required it. For example, how could anyone effectively run a railroad if people did not have an accurate idea of the time? How would anyone

The U.S. Naval Observatory in Washington, D.C., is in charge of maintaining the Department of Defense's standard for precise time. Here, two visitors observe the atomic clock.

know when a train was going to leave one station or arrive at another? In 1830, the U.S. Navy established the Depot of Charts and Instruments, which was later to become the U.S. Naval Observatory. Its main mission was to care for the U.S. Navy's chronometers, charts, and other navigational equipment and to keep the chronometers calibrated for accuracy. It was the start of one of the agency's main jobs: timekeeping.

In the 1840s, a railway standard time for Great Britain—England, Scotland, and Wales—was developed to replace the separate local time systems. In 1845, in the city of Washington, D.C., the U.S. Naval Observatory, at the request of the secretary of the navy, installed what was called a time ball on top of the dome of the observatory's telescope. Every day, precisely at noon, the time ball was dropped. This set the official time for people in Washington and for ships in the area that were setting out to sea. Thirty years later, a time ball atop the Western Union Building in New York City—then the tallest building in the city—was dropped by telegraphic signal from the Naval Observatory in Washington. This practical exercise was the precursor for the celebratory New Year's Eve ritual that millions of people worldwide now observe every year: the ball dropping in Times Square in New York City.

TIME ZONES

Because of its size, there are four time zones in the continental United States—Eastern, Central, Mountain, and Pacific. When it is 12:00 PM in the Eastern standard time (EST) zone, it is 11:00 AM in the Central standard time (CST) zone, 10:00 AM in the Mountain standard time (MST) zone, and 9:00 AM in the Pacific standard time (PST) zone. Because of its distance from the rest of the country, Alaska's time is an hour behind Pacific standard time, and Hawaii's time is two hours behind Pacific standard time.

Of all the large nations, only China does not use time zones. Because the whole country has only the one standard time, when it is light at noon in eastern China, it can be dark at noon in western China, since the sun hasn't risen there yet.

The Royal Observatory in Greenwich, England, began transmitting time telegraphically in 1852. By 1855, most of Britain was using what came to be known as Greenwich Mean (or standard) Time (GMT). A few clocks, like the large one on Tom Tower at Christ Church College, Oxford, were refitted with two hour hands, one for local time and one for GMT. Greenwich became important for timekeeping in a different way as well. Until the second half of the nineteenth century, no two countries used the same prime meridian, or starting point, for determining longitude. The Greenwich meridian became the most popular prime meridian, partly because of the reliability and correctness of the Greenwich Observatory's data and partly because the British Empire was so predominant around the world. In 1884, a conference was held in Washington, D.C. Forty-one delegates from twenty-five nations decided that the Greenwich meridian would be the prime meridian both for longitude and for keeping world time. The exact position of this meridian was marked by the position of the large Transit Circle telescope in the Greenwich Observatory's Meridian Building.

East and west of the Greenwich meridian, the world was divided into twenty-four time zones, matching the twenty-four hours in a day, though of course these zones can't be seen except on maps. However, in some countries, the borders of these zones aren't perfectly straight and follow national boundaries instead. In 1918, the U.S. government officially accepted Greenwich Mean Time and the Greenwich meridian as the standard timekeeping system, and the worldwide arrangement of time zones was accepted through an act of Congress.

As the United States grew and rail and telegraph lines were put in place, the Naval Observatory began its Time Service Department. This began just after the Civil War in 1865. A time signal was transmitted over telegraph lines to the Navy Department and activated the Washington fire bells at 7:00 AM, noon, and 6:00 PM. The service was sent across the nation via Western Union telegraph lines to give the railroads accurate time as well.

The railroad industry in the United States implemented the Standard Railway Time System in 1883. It was adopted by most—but not all—U.S. cities, and many people argued about it for years. The city of Detroit, Michigan, flatly refused to change from local time, which the city kept until 1900, when half of the city did switch to the standard system. The other half, though, still refused to change, and Detroit went back to its own local time. But in 1905, people gave up the fight, and Detroit joined the standard time of the rest of the country.

NINETEENTH- AND TWENTIETH-CENTURY BREAKTHROUGHS

In an experiment in 1880 that almost no one but scientists noticed, two Frenchmen, the brothers Pierre and Jacques Curie, discovered that if an electric field was applied to a quartz crystal, the crystal would vibrate. They called this effect piezoelectricity. For almost forty years, no one found a use for this effect, but it was going to play a large role in improved time-keeping in the modern age.

At the same time that standard time was being established, further innovations were producing better clocks. In 1889, a clock built by Siegmund Riefler had a nearly free pendulum that gave it accuracy within a hundredth of a second a day. This clock became the standard in many astronomical observatories. Nine years later, R. J. Rudd introduced a true free-pendulum clock. After this, several companies designed free-pendulum clocks.

The most important of the free-pendulum clocks was the W. H. Shortt clock. It appeared in 1921 and almost immediately replaced the Riefler clock in the observatories. The Shortt clock contained two pendulums, called by the names slave and master. The "slave" pendulum gave the "master" pendulum soft pushes to keep it in motion and drove the clock's hands as well. This kept the "master" pendulum free to do nothing but move with regular precision.

But the Shortt clock was quickly overtaken by something new in timekeeping. In 1927, a Canadian engineer named Warren Marrison, working for Bell

Laboratories in the United States, produced the first quartz clock. From the 1920s on, quartz clocks became more and more popular, since they offered much better performance than anything that had come before.

Quartz is a common mineral that is found in many types of rocks. It is also one of the hardest minerals and doesn't erode easily. There are many varieties: everything from amethyst and rose quartz, which are used in jewelry, to quartz sand and clear rock crystal. Quartz has many uses both in science and industry, and many of those are due to the piezoelectric effect that the Curies discovered in 1880. When a slice of quartz crystal is compressed, it develops a positive charge on one side and a negative charge on the other, like the positive and negative ends of a magnet. Electricity applied to a quartz crystal slice causes the slice to expand and contract, producing steady vibrations. Quartz crystal clocks have no gears or escapements that can wear out and cause inaccuracies.

In 1945, Isidor Rabi, a Columbia University physics professor, suggested that an even more accurate clock could be developed using a technique called atomic beam magnetic resonance, which used the natural vibrations of atoms instead of quartz crystals. Rabi's method worked. In 1949, the National

Use of the mineral quartz was a major step in making more accurate timepieces. Quartz crystals are still used in many watches and clocks today.

Bureau of Standards—now the National Institute of Standards and Technology—announced the world's first atomic clock, which used molecules of ammonia. It was less reliable than quartz clocks and was never used for timekeeping, but it was a working prototype, a model from which to start working on more practical designs.

Improvements in electronic technology, meanwhile, allowed quartz clocks to be made smaller. By 1961, portable quartz clocks were being produced, and quartz crystals were—and still are—being used in most wristwatches. Today, quartz clocks and watches can be found everywhere because they provide very good performance for a low price.

ATOMIC CLOCKS

Through the 1960s, both the National Bureau of Standards in the United States and the National Physical Laboratory in England worked on developing more and more advanced atomic clocks, using the element cesium. The container of an atomic clock holds a microwave radio transmitter, which gives off a steady series of high-frequency radio waves, like a miniature radar set. When the radio waves hit the cesium atoms, the atoms absorb them and give off light. A photocell, which is like the electric eye sensor in a modern door, tracks the light. Whenever the light gets dimmer, the photocell sends a signal to the radio transmitter, which adjusts its frequency. A counter reads the radio waves generated by the transmitter. A computer translates the numbers from the counter into a readable signal that looks like the reading from a digital clock.

By 1964, atomic clocks had reached an accuracy of within one second in six thousand years. Since

When the cesium atomic clock was developed in 1955, it was the most accurate clock in the world. This early atomic clock is accurate to one second in three hundred years.

cesium atoms were proving themselves so dependable, the cesium atom's natural frequency, or rate of vibration, was accepted in 1967 as the new international unit of time. A second was defined as exactly 9,192,631,770 oscillations, or ticks, of the cesium atom. In 1972, Coordinated Universal Time (UTC) was adopted as the official time for the world. The Bureau International des Poids et Mesures, or International Bureau of Weights and Measures, in Paris acts as the official timekeeper of atomic time for the world. Over fifty laboratories around the world with around two hundred atomic clocks are used to calculate this complex measurement.

Atomic clock design is still being refined. By the 1990s, atomic clocks were accurate to within one second in six million years. Today's cesium fountain atomic clocks are thought to be off by less than one second every fifty million years.

GPS

One use of precise timing is in the pinpointing of locations. The Global Positioning System, or GPS, is a network of satellites, each carrying three atomic clocks. The United States, Russia, and China each

Aim
Provide precise geographic positioning data for planes, boats, vehicles and individuals equipped with a receptor

Each satellite emits a **coded radio signal**

The system **calculates latitude, longitude and time** using signals from at least 4 satellites

Communications centre on the ground syncronises the signals

Possible uses include: guidance systems, border controls, locating vehicles, finding directions at sea and in mountains

This diagram shows how a GPS device communicates with at least four satellites to pinpoint its geographic location.

have GPS satellites orbiting the earth, and the European Union is also launching its own GPS. A GPS unit on the ground, in the air, or at sea receives radio signals from at least four of these satellites and, after measuring the time it takes for the radio signals to travel, it can accurately calculate its location. During construction of the tunnel under the English Channel,

British and French crews started digging from opposite ends and used GPS receivers to make sure they met up perfectly in the middle. Although GPS was originally used by the U.S. Department of Defense, it is now used by just about everybody: police and fire departments, scientists tracking endangered animals, and even commuters driving to work. GPS units are small, handheld devices, and GPS capabilities are standard in most cell phones.

"Spring Forward" and "Fall Back"

Daylight saving time is a system in which clocks are set one hour forward at a certain date in the spring to allow one more hour of daylight and, technically, save electricity by reducing evening use of lights by an hour. The clocks are then set back one hour at a certain date in the autumn. In the United States, daylight saving time always begins on the second Sunday in March and ends on the first Sunday in November. Not all states follow daylight saving time. Arizona, Hawaii, and Indiana do not.

Some countries went to daylight saving time during a time of war, when energy needed to be conserved. Both Britain and the United States adopted such a plan during World War I (1914–1918) and again during World War II (1939–1945). But after 1945, many countries kept daylight saving time. In the United States, the official policy began in 1967. Daylight saving time begins on the second Sunday in March. Then beginning in 2007, daylight saving time was extended by four weeks to its current timeframe. In Europe, the daylight saving period is called the summer time period.

TIME IN MODERN TIMES

Chapter
4

I n the twenty-first century, we recognize many different concepts of time. In physics, time is one of the fundamental properties of the universe, like length and mass and electric charge. Material objects not only have mass and spatial dimensions, but they exist at or for certain lengths of time, and in the most advanced studies of the cosmos, time is considered another dimension. In fact, time actually cannot be considered separately from the other dimensions, and physicists speak of the conjoined phenomena space-time. It is known that the universe is expanding, so space and time appear to move together.

Time, it should be noted, moves in only one direction, forward, never backward, a consequence of the laws of thermodynamics, which state that heat energy can move in only one direction, from higher to lower temperatures.

THE FORWARD FLOW OF TIME

The forward flow of time is sometimes called time's arrow, and it is determined by the thermodynamic principle of entropy, or increasing disorder. If the universe continues to expand, scientists have to consider the possibility that eventually all the potential heat energy stored in matter will be evenly distributed throughout the universe. That energy will then be unavailable; that is, it can no longer be made to flow from one place to another because there will be no temperature differentials anywhere in the cosmos. Physical processes caused by the transfer of heat energy will cease, and this is called the "heat death" of the universe.

Scientists have always wondered, and continue to wonder, about the origin of the universe, including the origin of time. How did time begin? The question has been answered with a theory known as the

big bang model of the universe. The theory states that about twelve to fourteen billion years ago, all the matter in the entire universe was crammed into an unimaginably small space. A sudden powerful explosion occurred, and the hot, dense mass of the universe-to-be was thrown apart, expanding outward in all directions. Time began with that primordial explosion and continued as the new universe began to evolve into stars, planets, and everything else.

Did time exist before the big bang? This is a problematic question for scientists because they work only with measurable quantities. Time can be measured by the rate or speed at which objects change position or the way that events succeed each other. As the universe expands and the distances between objects change at measurable rates, we can comprehend the notion of time. Before the universe existed, before there was any space in which objects could move, the notion of time is difficult to define.

The European Space Agency (ESA) launched the Planck satellite in 2009. The straylight shield, shown here, is one component of the satellite that will help scientists study radiation from the big bang. For this reason, the Planck satellite has been dubbed the ESA's "time machine."

STEPHEN HAWKING

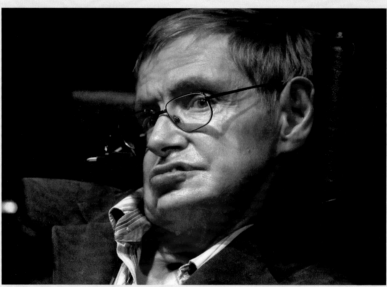

Stephen Hawking continues to give public lectures on various scientific topics. Here, he is speaking to a sold-out auditorium at the University of California, Berkeley, in 2007.

Theoretical physicist and cosmologist Stephen Hawking was born in 1942 in Oxford, England. Hawking is best known for his work in cosmology, especially in the study of black holes.

Hawking received his undergraduate education in physics at University College in Oxford, England. In the 1960s, he began his studies of cosmology at Cambridge. Hawking was stricken with amyotrophic lateral sclerosis, or Lou

Gehrig's disease, a degenerative neurological condition that causes paralysis and muscle atrophy, or wasting away. But Hawking never let his condition keep him from his work.

In 1988, Hawking published *A Brief History of Time: From the Big Bang to Black Holes*. The goal of this book was to explain difficult concepts of cosmology and the universe to readers who did not necessarily have a strong background in science. The record-breaking book was on the London *Sunday Times* best-seller list for more than four years and has since been republished in several different editions. Because of his popularity, he has been referred to as a "celebrity scientist." In 2001, Hawking released *The Universe in a Nutshell*, which tries to explain the nature of time and string theory in a clear, easy to understand manner.

Hawking continues to do research and public lectures. His latest book, *The Grand Design*, was released in September 2010.

Albert Einstein's Theories

In the first decades of the twentieth century, the way scientists looked at time and space was changed forever. The reason for such a major change was the appearance of two theories, the special and general theories of relativity, both created by Albert Einstein. Born in Germany in 1879, he was the most important physicist of the twentieth century and certainly one of the greatest and most famous scientists of all time.

In 1900, after his graduation from a university in Zurich, Switzerland, Einstein spent two years looking for work. He finally settled for a job at the patent office in Bern, Switzerland, where he worked from 1902 to 1909, reviewing patent applications for new inventions. This was a routine job, not one that needed much attention for someone as sharp as Einstein, and it allowed him a great deal of free time for thinking about physics.

Einstein was struck by an idea, which he wrote up in 1905 as the special theory of relativity. In it, he stated, among other things, that time is not absolute. What this means is that the measurement of time depends on where someone is and how fast that person is moving in relation to the objects he or she is observing. Only the speed of light, Einstein wrote, is always the same. For the speed of light to remain constant for all observers, both distance and time would have to change to keep everything

Albert Einstein won the Nobel Prize in Physics in 1921. He lectured throughout America, Europe, and the Far East during the 1920s. Einstein was awarded memberships, fellowships, and honorary degrees in universities all over the world.

balanced. Einstein showed that how fast time moves depends on how fast the clock measuring that time is moving. The faster the clock is being physically moved, the more slowly time passes for that clock, as measured by an observer who is not moving with that clock. Astronauts traveling out into space and back to the earth on a very fast spaceship, one able to move close to the speed of light, would find themselves faced with an odd problem. They might have spent only five years in space, from their point of view, but on the earth, about thirty years might have passed. While in their swift ship, the passage of time would appear to pass at the same rate, but when they returned to the earth, they would not have aged as much as those they left behind.

Einstein also showed that the faster an object went, the more mass it acquired—the more resistant it became to further changes in its motion—and therefore the more energy it needed to be pushed even faster. To go faster than the speed of light was impossible, since it would take an infinite amount of energy to push an infinitely massive object.

In 1906, Einstein's former college teacher in mathematics, Hermann Minkowski (1864–1909), came up with a new idea for considering space and time. Space and time were to be combined into a new physical entity called space-time. The mathematics of relativity revealed that space and time had to be combined

Hermann Minkowski's model for the four-dimensional
space-time continuum laid the mathematical basis for
Einstein's special theory of relativity.

if the equations are to accurately describe what we
see. Because space has three dimensions—height,
width, and depth—and time has one dimension, our
universe has to be, at a minimum, four-dimensional.
Scientists now consider our world and everything
around it to be part of a four-dimensional space-time
continuum (a sequence or progression).

What does it mean to say that an object has a
certain number of dimensions? It means that it takes

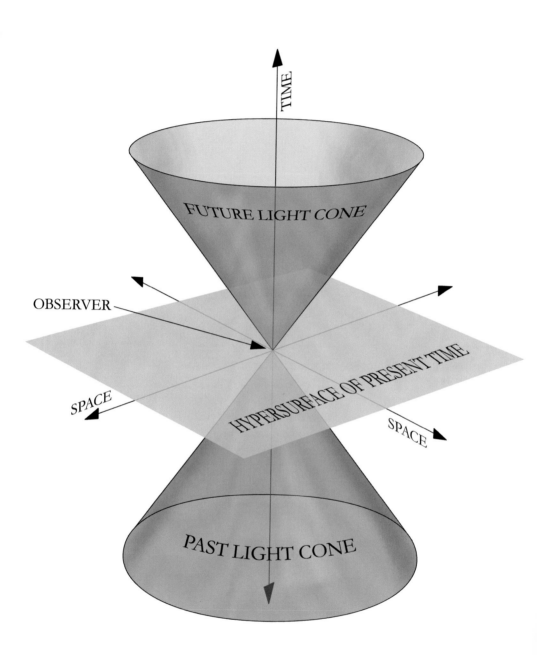

a certain number of coordinates, or numbers, to describe the physical properties of that object. To locate an object in space, using any other point as a reference, we need to specify three numbers, equivalent to length, width, and depth. But because objects are in motion, we also have to specify a fourth number, representing when the object exists.

In a research paper published in 1916, Einstein, with his general theory of relativity, showed that gravity could bend light. His claim was proved three years later during a 1919 solar eclipse, when British astronomer Arthur S. Eddington (1882–1944) detected the bending of starlight by the sun's enormous gravitational field. Einstein also showed that gravity could affect time. The gravitational field of a massive object like the earth should cause clocks closer to the object to appear to run slower, just as if they were accelerating to high velocities.

In 1962, two atomic clocks that scientists mounted at the top and bottom of a water tower provided a chance to test Einstein's theory about time and gravity. Sure enough, Einstein was right. The clock at the bottom of the tower, closer to the center of

This diagram, known as the Minkowski space-time cone, is a representation of the four dimensions of space-time. In this model, the observer is positioned at the center of the diagram between the past and the future.

WHAT IS A BLACK HOLE?

The equations of Einstein's general theory also predict the existence of what scientists call black holes. If gravity can bend light, it is conceivable that the region of space surrounding a very massive object would experience a gravitational force so strong that light rays bend completely around the object and no light can escape from that region. The distance from such a massive object where light turns on itself is called the event horizon. Within this horizon, we see nothing and can obtain no information about what is happening. At the event horizon, to distant observers, time slows to a standstill. A black hole can form when a massive star runs out of its nuclear fuel and its core collapses in on itself, crushed by its own gravitational force. If the star's core has enough mass, the collapse continues until all that mass is concentrated at a tiny point in its center, possibly smaller than the nucleus of an atom. Physicists call this point a singularity. Within that singularity, we have no conception of what is happening to the material objects trapped there. All we know is that the mass is still there because of the continuing presence of a powerful gravitational field.

Though no light escapes from inside the event horizon, black holes are not entirely invisible. Just outside the event horizon, the matter falling inward is subjected to such tremendous forces that it begins to give off intense radiation. There are thought to be many black holes throughout our galaxy, and one of the ways we try to detect them is by looking in the sky for regions of space that give off large numbers of gamma rays or X-rays. These spots of intense radiation indicate that powerful forces are at work in these regions, though we may detect no objects like stars there.

the earth's mass, did appear to run more slowly than the clock at the top of the tower. Many other experiments have since demonstrated the correctness of Einstein's theory. Scientists have measured the rates of decay of subatomic particles entering the earth's atmosphere as cosmic rays at speeds close to the speed of light. These particles appear to take longer to decay, or transform themselves into other particles, than in laboratory experiments where the particles are not moving so fast.

TRAVELING THROUGH TIME

But if time can be slowed down, can it also run backward? Is time travel to the past really possible?

Time travel was an established part of science fiction even before Einstein proposed his theories. British author H. G. Wells wrote his famous novel *The Time Machine* in 1895. But modern scientists are very skeptical of such an idea. As mentioned, the known laws of thermodynamics require that the energy in a closed system flows in one direction only. If objects or people could remove themselves from one time frame and move to another, all sorts of contradictions would arise between the causes of events and their effects. That would mean abandoning most of the principles of modern science. And where could one go in the past? The universe is in motion, and the earth and the stars and the galaxies no longer exist in the space-time where they existed yesterday. Movement in time appears to be different from linear movement through the other dimensions, and explaining how it might occur requires enormous complications to known science that have little experimental justification.

And yet, in the 1980s, astronomer Carl Sagan (1934–1996) was working on a science fiction novel. For purposes of the plot, he wanted his characters to be able to use a shortcut through space by traveling from earth through a black hole to a distant world. This wouldn't be possible by the accepted rules of physics, particularly since the intense gravity within a black hole would crush anything that came near it.

So Sagan asked a fellow scientist and friend, theoretical physicist Kip S. Thorne (1940–), for advice. Working as a professor at the California Institute of Technology, Thorne carries out research on black holes and the nature of space, time, and gravity.

Einstein had pondered the idea of a wormhole as early as 1913. Now Thorne would refine it. A wormhole was thought to be a kind of tunnel through space-time created by a black hole, linking distant parts of the universe. Matter would fall in, but instead of being crushed into a singularity, it would somehow be transported to a different region of space. Sagan finished his novel, *Contact*, in 1985, and it was made into a movie in 1997. Later, Thorne speculated that a wormhole could also be used to travel backward in time. A wormhole that takes a shortcut through space-time could just as easily link two different times as two different places. Thorne has been studying the subject of wormholes ever since.

Are there such wormholes anywhere in the space-time continuum? It is pure speculation that such phenomena exist. Mathematical equations say that wormholes are at least possible. Can we use them to travel across space or through time? Right now, the answer is apparently not. According to the equations, if wormholes really do exist, they would be too small and unstable for any safe use. It looks as though travel through wormholes is indeed science fiction.

The laws of causality make some people argue that time travel simply won't work. They mention the "grandfather paradox" as a case in point. In this scenario, you go back in time, and for whatever reason, you kill your grandfather. But when you kill him, you end your family history and cease to exist. You therefore aren't around to go back to kill your grandfather. Resolving such conundrums seems impossible if time travel can actually occur.

There's another interesting argument from those who think time travel is impossible. They say that if it is possible, we should already have met time travelers from the future. In fact, our entire world should already have been turned upside down by the interference and changes caused by visitors from the future. But if that were true, would we know it? With each change to the past, history would be rewritten, along with our memories and experiences. We would wake up each day, so to speak, with no knowledge that we had lived differently yesterday. In that case, our memories are illusory. One can begin to see the enormous difficulties in the recording and measurement of the physical world, in our faith in

Director Robert Zemeckis adapted Carl Sagan's novel *Contact* into a feature film starring Jodie Foster as astronomer Ellie Arroway.

This conceptual representation of a wormhole is just one artist's interpretation of how this hypothetical portal might appear tearing through space-time.

the continuity of our experiences, and in the foundations of science as we understand them, if time travel were possible. This makes it very distasteful to most scientists.

On the Cutting Edge

In the level of quantum, however, the microscopic level at which we examine the behavior of subatomic particles, some experiments have been conducted whose results seem to imply that the laws of causality can be violated. These subtle experiments seem to be telling us that under some circumstances, information can be transmitted faster than the speed of light, or a single subatomic particle can exist in two places at once. Theoretical calculations have led to the concept of the tachyon, a hypothetical particle that cannot move slower than the speed of light and that moves backward in time as soon as it is created. But such experiments and calculations are on the very cutting edge of physics, and we are not at all sure what their results mean or what they are telling us about the physical world. For all of humankind's time spent obsessing over time, it's clear we still have much to learn.

12 to 14 billion years ago The big bang occurs: the universe goes from a very hot and dense state and expands very quickly.

3000 BCE Sumerians in Mesopotamia create a twelve-month calendar.

1100 BCE Egyptians create a catalog of what they can see of the universe with the naked eye.

1286 A clock is installed in St. Paul's Cathedral in London.

14th century CE The first mechanical clocks appear in towers in Italian cities.

16th century Spring-powered clocks are developed. Peter Henlein is credited as the inventor of the pocket watch.

1506 Pedro Reinel is the first person to draw latitude lines on the map.

1582 The Gregorian calendar is created and is still in use in the Western world today.

1656 Christian Huygens patents the world's first pendulum clock.

1657 Robert Hooke designs and patents the first anchor escapement.

1675 King Charles II of England founds the Royal Observatory in Greenwich, England, to find a way to keep track of the time aboard ships as they pass through different longitudes.

1830 The U.S. Navy establishes the Depot of Charts and Instruments in Washington, D.C. (later to become the U.S. Naval Observatory).

1852 The Royal Observatory begins transmitting time by telegraph.

1859 Charles Darwin publishes *The Origin of Species*, proposing his theory of evolution and stating that most evolutionary change was gradual, requiring millions or billions of years. Darwin's theory helped support contemporaries' theories on the age of the earth.

1865 The U.S. Naval Observatory began its Time Service Department following the Civil War.

1889 Siegmund Riefler builds a clock with a nearly free pendulum with accuracy within a hundredth of a second a day. This clock became the standard in many astronomical observatories.

1898 R. J. Rudd introduces a true free-pendulum clock.

1905 Albert Einstein publishes his special theory of relativity.

1906 Hermann Minkowski introduces the concept of the space-time continuum based on Einstein's special theory of relativity.

1916 Einstein publishes his general theory of relativity.

1921 The two-pendulum W. H. Shortt clock replaces the Riefler clock in observatories.

1927 Warren Marrison makes the first quartz clock.

1949 The first atomic clock is made.

1967 The United States' first nonwartime daylight saving policy is enacted.

1972 Coordinated Universal Time (UTC) is adopted as the official time for the world.

2008 National Institute of Standards and Technology (NIST) physicists develop a quantum logic clock using individual aluminum and mercury ions, creating the most accurate clocks to date.

2010 NIST scientists, using a single aluminum atom, build an enhanced version of the quantum logic clock that neither gains nor loses a second in over two billion years.

Glossary

atomic clock An extremely precise timekeeping
  device based on the natural vibrations of cesium
  atoms or other chemical elements.

big bang A theory of the start of the universe
  that states that all matter was compressed
  into a tiny point billions of years ago and
  then expanded.

black hole An extremely small region of space-
  time, possibly a collapsed massive star,
  with a gravitational field from which nothing
  can escape.

calendar A device for keeping track of days,
  weeks, months, and years.

catastrophism The idea that the earth's features
  had been created suddenly in a series of rapid
  cataclysmic events, like floods.

Coordinated Universal Time (UTC) The international time standard.

daylight saving time A system that adds an hour
  of daylight by moving clocks forward an hour in
  the spring. Clocks are then moved back an hour
  in autumn.

equinox The date or time, occurring twice
  every year, where the day and night are
  equal length.

geology The scientific study of the earth and its
  rocks and minerals.

Greenwich Mean Time The standard time on which the world's time is based; also called universal time.

latitude The imaginary lines running east to west, dividing up the globe in horizontal segments.

longitude The imaginary lines running north to south on the globe that are the important dividers of local times.

nomad A person who wanders from one place to another in search of food or shelter.

orrery A mechanical model of the solar system showing the relative positions of the sun and planets as time passes.

pendulum A weight that is hung and swings freely to regulate the mechanism of a clock.

prime meridian Passing through Greenwich, London, England, the prime meridian is set as zero longitude.

radiometric dating A method of finding the age of something by measuring the radioactive decay of its isotopes.

rudimentary Early or primitive, limited to basic principles.

solstice Occurring every year, the winter and summer solstices mark the shortest and longest days of the year, respectively.

space-time continuum The universe and everything in it, in which time and space are joined.

theory A scientific idea or concept based on as much factual information as possible and devised to explain the nature or behavior of something.

time machine In fiction, a machine that lets someone travel backward or forward in time.

time zone An area of land that falls within a range of longitudes where a common standard time is observed. There are four time zones in the continental United States.

water clock A rudimentary device that measures time by the regulated dropping of water from one vessel to another.

wormhole A hypothetical tunnel created by a black hole that links different places in the space-time continuum.

Canadian Clock Museum

60 James Street

Deep River, ON K0J 1P0

Canada

(613) 584-9687

Web site: http://www.canclockmuseum.ca

This nonprofit museum is Canada's sole clock museum. It is dedicated to the history and display of Canada's many clock manufacturers, from the early nineteenth century to the present day.

International Bureau of Weights and Measures

Pavillon de Breteuil

F-92312 Sèvres Cedex

France

Web site: http://www.bipm.org/en/home

Created in 1875, this French organization is one of three international standards organizations tasked with maintaining the International System of Units. One of its important tasks is to maintain a worldwide time and create the single, official coordinated universal time (UTC).

National Association of Watch and Clock Collectors

514 Poplar Street

Columbia, PA 17512

(717) 684-8261

Web site: http://www.nawcc.org

The National Association of Watch and Clock Collectors, founded in 1943, is an organization comprised of hobbyists, collectors, students, and teachers who all share an interest in the science of timekeeping.

National Institute of Standards and Technology Physics Laboratory

100 Bureau Drive, M/S 8400
Gaithersburg, MD 20899-8400
(301) 975-4200
Web site: http://www.nist.gov/physlab
A unit of the National Institute of Standards and Technology, the Physics Laboratory conducts research on many different levels of the physical sciences, with research geared to fit the needs of industry, government, and academia in the United States.

School of Horology

514 Poplar Street
Columbia, PA 17512
(717) 684-8261
Web site: http://www.horology.edu
Part of the National Association of Watch and Clock Collectors, the School of Horology is a leader in watch and clock repair and education.

U.S. Naval Observatory

3450 Massachusetts Avenue NW
Washington, DC 20392-5420

(202) 762-1467

Web site: http://www.usno.navy.mil/USNO

The mission of the U.S. Naval Observatory includes both monitoring the motion of celestial bodies and issuing the official time to the U.S. Department of Defense. The facility also hosts tours, by reservation, to showcase the Master Clock system and explain the responsibilities of the U.S. Naval Observatory.

WEB SITES

Due to the changing nature of Internet links, Rosen Publishing has developed an online list of Web sites related to the subject of this book. This site is updated regularly. Please use this link to access the list:

http://www.rosenlinks.com/phys/time

Bankston, John. *Stephen Hawking: Breaking the Boundaries of Time and Space*. Berkeley Heights, NJ: Enslow Publishers, 2005.

Collier, James Lincoln. *Clocks*. New York, NY: Benchmark Books, 2009.

Daniels, George. *Watchmaking*. London, England: Philip Wilson Publishers, 2010.

Goldberg, Dave, and Jeff Blomquist. *A User's Guide to the Universe: Surviving the Perils of Black Holes, Time Paradoxes, and Quantum Uncertainty*. Hoboken, NJ: John Wiley & Sons, 2010.

Goldenstern, Joyce. *Albert Einstein: Physicist and Genius*. Berkeley Heights, NJ: Enslow Publishers, 2008.

Gow, Mary. *Robert Hooke: Creative Genius, Scientist, Inventor*. Berkeley Heights, NJ: Enslow Publishers, 2006.

Hawking, Stephen. *A Brief History of Time*. New York, NY: Bantam Books, 1998.

Jenkins, Martin. *The Time Book: A Brief History from Lunar Calendars to Atomic Clocks*. Somerville, MA: Candlewick, Press, 2009.

Kelly, Harold C. *Clock Repairing as a Hobby: An Illustrated How-To Guide for the Beginner*. New York, NY: Skyhorse Publishing, 2007.

Kirkland, Kyle. *Time and Thermodynamics*. New York, NY: Facts On File, 2007.

Major, F. G. *The Quantum Beat: Principles and Applications of Atomic Clocks*. New York, NY: Springer, 2009.

Mara, Wil. *The Clock*. New York, NY: Children's Press, 2006.

Rand, Casey. *Time*. Chicago, IL: Heinemann Library, 2011.

Randles, Jenny. *Breaking the Time Barrier: The Race to Build the First Time Machine*. New York, NY: Paraview Pocket Books, 2005.

Raum, Elizabeth. *The Story Behind Time*. Chicago, IL: Heinemann Library, 2009.

Sobel, Dava. *Longitude: The True Story of a Lone Genius Who Solved the Greatest Scientific Problem of His Time*. New York, NY: Walker & Company, 2007.

Thorne, Kip S. *Black Holes and Time Warps: Einstein's Outrageous Legacy*. W. W. Norton & Company, 1994.

Tyson, Neil deGrasse. *Death by Black Hole: And Other Cosmic Quandaries*. New York, NY: W. W. Norton & Company, 2007.

Wells, H. G. *The Time Machine*. Philadelphia, PA: Copper Penny Press, 2008.

T

U

V

W

Y

About the Authors

Johnny Kagayame is a writer who lives in Boise, Idaho, with his dogs Nordstrom, Paulo, and Scrappy.

Josepha Sherman is a professional author with more than 40 books and 125 stories and articles in print.

Photo Credits

Cover, interior graphics, pp. 4, 22-23, 50-51, 66-67 Shutterstock; pp. 8–9 Erich Lessing/Art Resource, NY; pp. 12–13, 17, 46, 69 Science & Society Picture Library/ SSPL/Getty Images; p. 19 © Hoberman Collection/ SuperStock; p. 28 Manuel Cohen/Getty Image News/ Getty Images; p. 32 Folb/Hulton Archive/Getty Images; pp. 38, 42–43 © SSPL/The Image Works; p. 45 Jamie Cooper/SSPL/Getty Images; p. 53 Library of Congress Prints and Photographs Division; pp. 58–59 Michael Smith/Getty Images News/Getty Images; p. 71 Newscom; p. 76 ESA/Getty Images News/Getty Images; p. 78 Justin Sullivan/Getty Images News/Getty Images; p. 81 Keystone/Hulton Archive/Getty Images; pp. 83, 84 SPL/ Photo Researchers; p. 90 Getty Images Entertainment/ Getty Images; pp. 92–93 Julian Baum/Photo Researchers.

Photo Researcher: Marty Levick